THE COMBAT HISTORY OF THE *21. PANZER DIVISION*

Map Book

Werner Kortenhaus

Translated, edited and revised by Frederick P. Steinhardt, MS, PhD.

Assistant editor Derick Hammond

Helion & Company

Helion & Company Limited
Unit 8 Amherst Business Centre
Budbrooke Road
Warwick
CV34 5WE
England
Tel. 01926 499 619
Fax 0121 711 4075
Email: info@helion.co.uk
Website: www.helion.co.uk
Twitter: @helionbooks
Visit our blog http://blog.helion.co.uk/

Published by Helion & Company 2014. Reprinted in paperback 2018
Designed and typeset by Mach 3 Solutions Ltd (www.mach3solutions.co.uk)
Cover designed by Paul Hewitt, Battlefield Design (www.battlefield-design.co.uk)

This English edition © Helion & Company 2014. Translated, edited and revised by
Frederick P. Steinhardt, MS, PhD.
Originally published as: *21. Panzerdivision 1943-1945*.
German edition © Schneider Armour Research 2007. All rights reserved.

⌬chneĭder
Armour Research

Images © as indicated within book.
Maps © Helion & Company 2014. Maps drawn by George Anderson.

ISBN 978-1-912174-14-0

Front cover: *Panzerjäger Marder* I, 7.5 cm Pak 40 L/46, based on the Hotchkiss H 39 (Bundesarchiv,
Bild 101I-493-3365-20). Rear cover: Once again the main burden of the fighting and sacrifices fell
on the infantryman. He also kept permanent lookout for ground-attack aircraft (Bundesarchiv, Bild
101I-299-1815-3). Front cover: Panzerjäger Marder I, 7.5 cm Pak 40 L/46, based on the Hotchkiss
H 39 (Bundesarchiv, Bild 101I-493-3365-20). Rear cover: Once again the main burden of the
fighting and sacrifices fell on the infantryman. He also kept permanent lookout for ground-attack
aircraft (Bundesarchiv, Bild 101I-299-1815-3).

British Library Cataloguing-in-Publication Data
A catalogue record for this book is available from the British Library

For details of other military history titles published by Helion & Company Limited contact the
above address, or visit our website: http://www.helion.co.uk

We always welcome receiving book proposals from prospective authors working in military history.

Contents

Map Key

Symbol	Label	Symbol	Label	Symbol	Label
	Army		Panzer Grenadier Battalion		Anti-Aircraft gun in position
	Panzer Corps		Panzer Grenadier Battalion		Anti-Aircraft Gun
	Panzer Division		Panzer Grenadier Company		Motorised Anti-Aircraft Battalion
	Panzer Brigade		Panzer Engineer Company		Artillery Regiment
	Panzer Regiment		Motorised Infantry Battalion		Artillery Battalion
	Panzer Company		Infantry Division		Artillery in position
	Panzer Artillery Regiment		Infantry Company		Motorised Artillery Battalion
	Self-Propelled Art. Company		Motorised Infantry Company		50/75mm Infantry Gun
	Panzer Reconnaissance Battalion		Engineer Battalion		Towed Artillery
	Panzer Vehicle Park		Motorised Engineer Battalion		Howitzer
	Panzer Engineer Battalion		Fallschirmjäger Division		Heavy Artillery
	Assault Gun		Towed Anti-Tank Battalion		Towed Rocket Launcher Battalion
	Panzer		Towed Anti-Tank Gun		Motorised Rocket Launcher Battalion
	Panzer Grenadier Division		Towed Rocket Launcher		Self-Propelled Artillery
	Panzer Grenadier Regiment		Anti-Aircraft Regiment		Armoured/Concrete Gun under Construction
	Panzer Grenadier Regiment		Towed Anti-Aircraft Gun		

	Paratroops		Armoured Battalion		Infantry Regiment
	Armoured Division		Armoured Company		Infantry Battalion
	Armoured Brigade		Infantry Division		Reconnaissance Regiment
	Armoured Regiment		Infantry Brigade		Airborne Division

	Beach Defences		Railway		Front Lines
	Maginot Line		Defences		Light Defences
	Waterlogged		Forest		Casemates

List of Maps

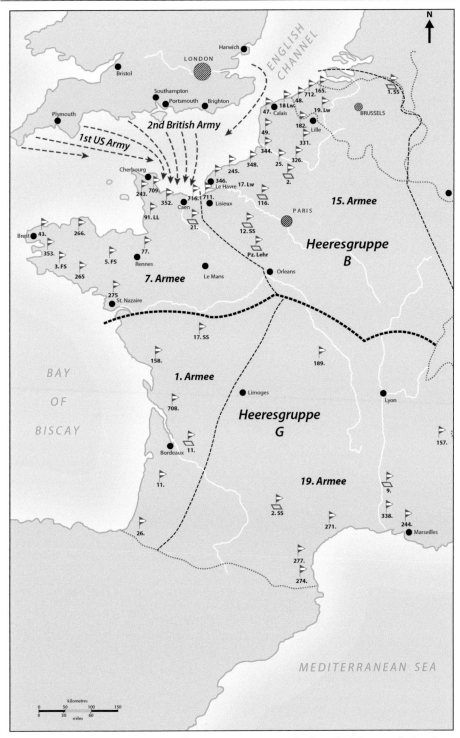

1. Location of principal German formations in France before the Normandy landings

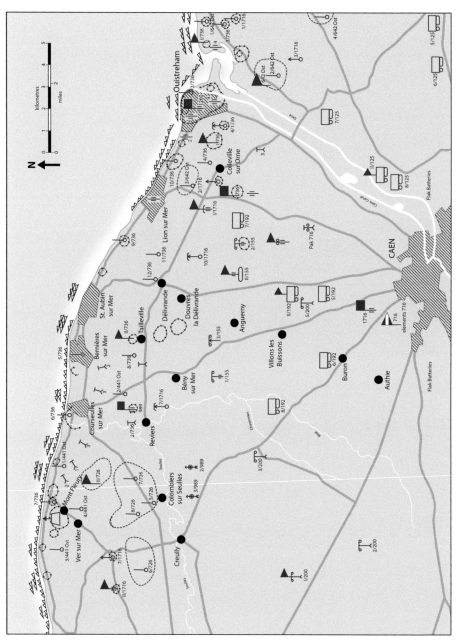

2. German formations between Ver-sur-Mer and Franceville

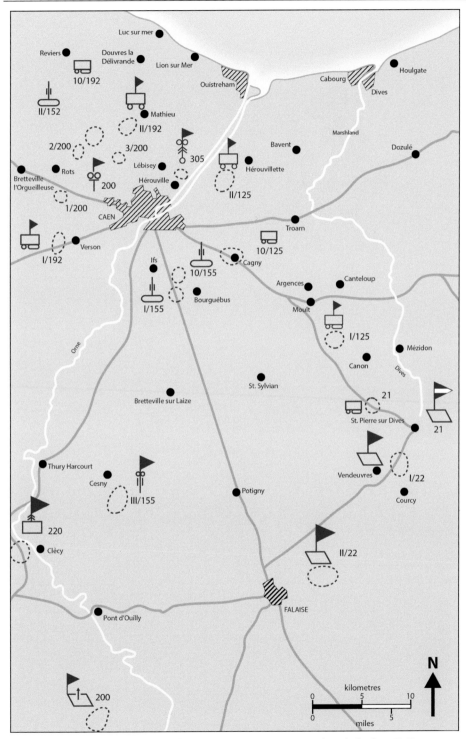

3. Location of the units of *21. Panzer Division* immediately before D-Day

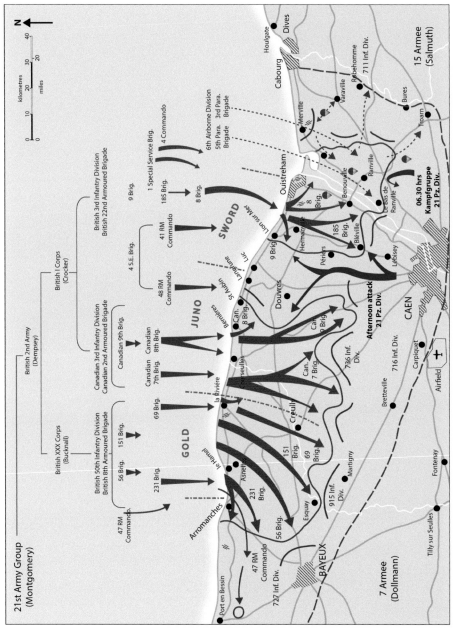

4. British and Canadian landings and formations during the first days of the Normandy campaign

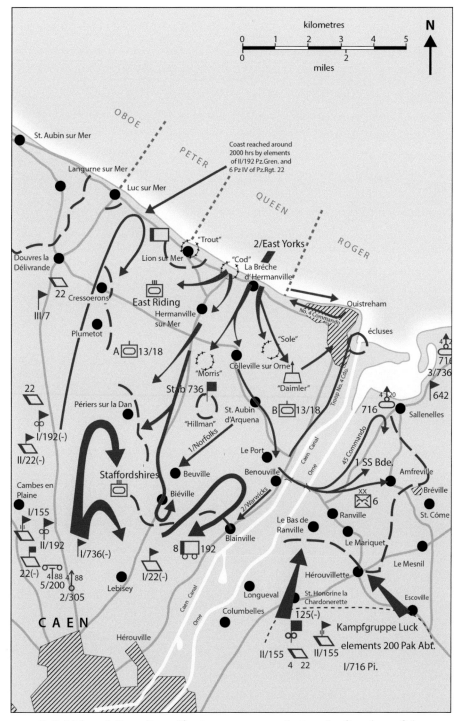

5. British and Canadian offensive movements during the first days of the
Normandy campaign and German counter-attacks

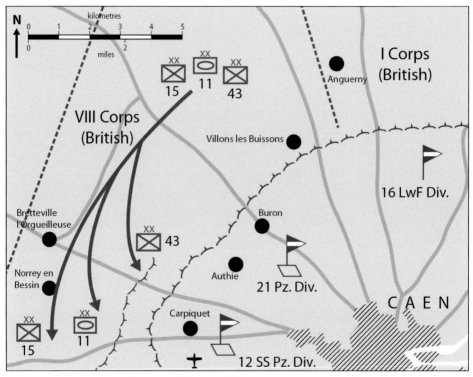

6. Operation "Epsom", beginning 25 June 1944

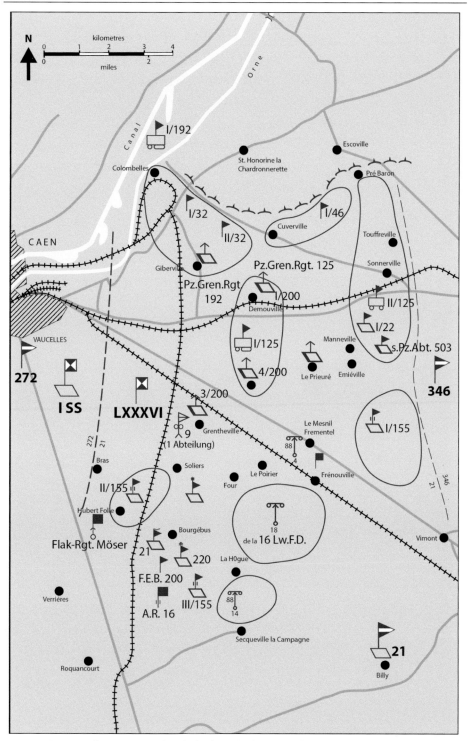

7. German forces immediately before the launch of Operation "Goodwood"

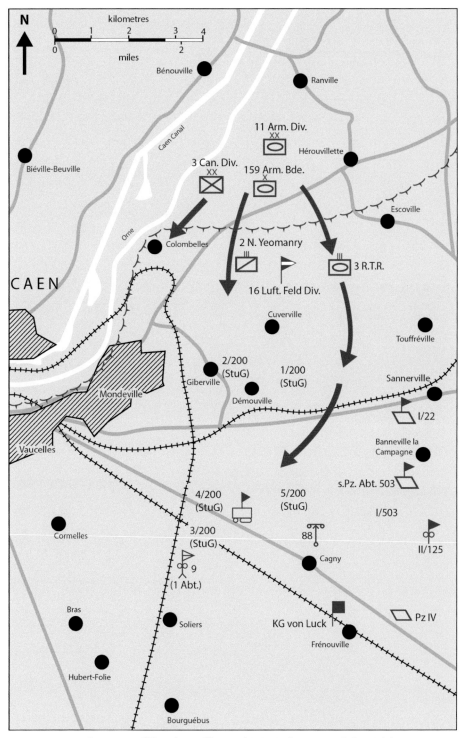

8. Operation "Goodwood" – 0745-0920 hours, 18 July 1944

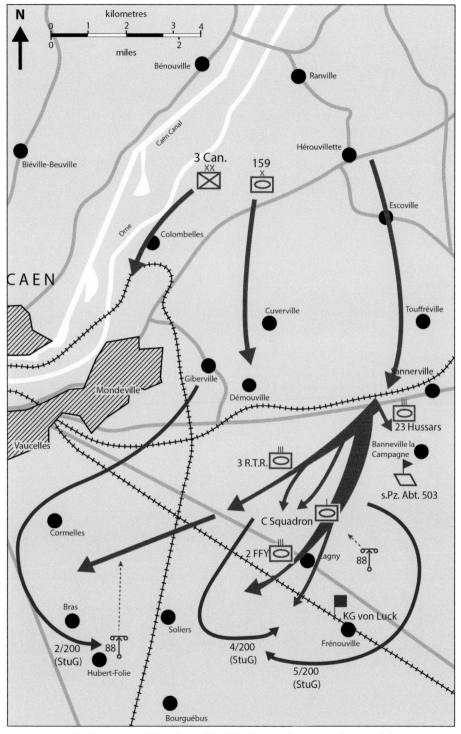

9. Operation "Goodwood" – 0920-1100 hours, 18 July 1944

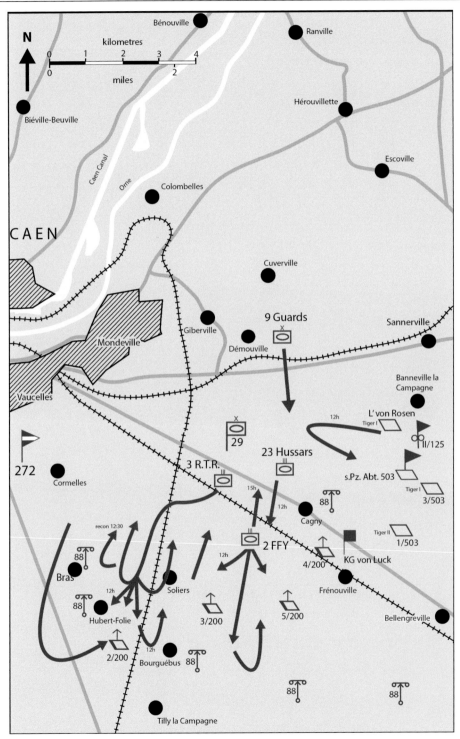

10. Operation "Goodwood" – 1100-1500 hours, 18 July 1944

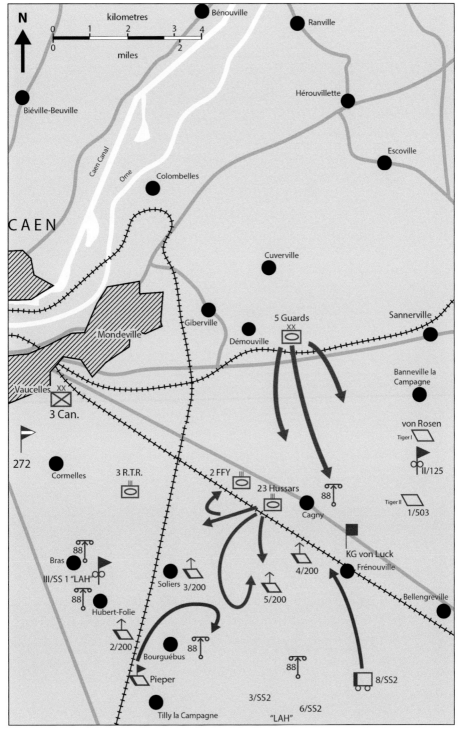

11. Operation "Goodwood" – 1500-1900 hours, 18 July 1944

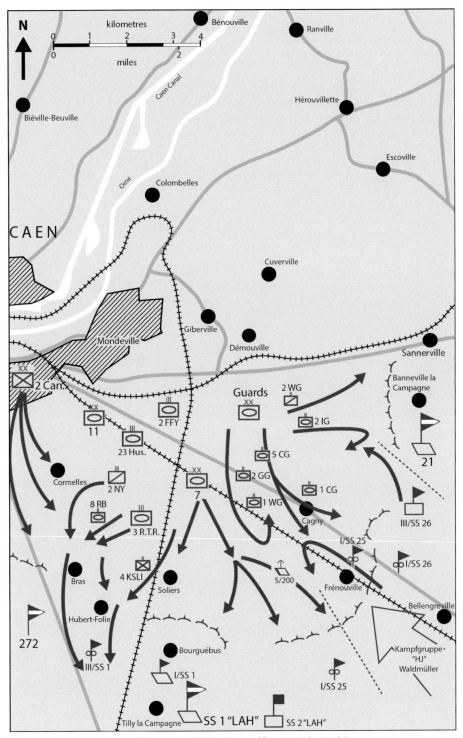

12. Operation "Goodwood" – 19 July 1944

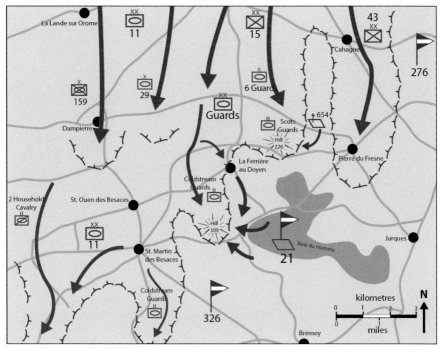

13. *21. Panzer Division* during Operation "Bluecoat", 30 July-1 August 1944

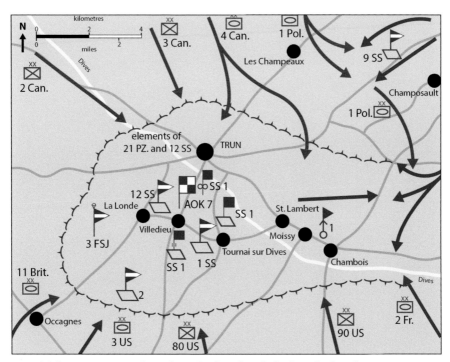

14. The situation in the Falaise Pocket shortly before the break-out attempt

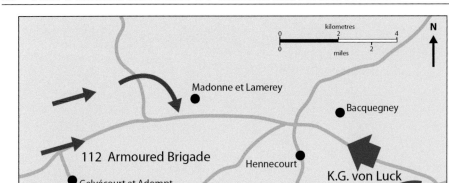

15. The counter-attack of *Panzerbrigade 112* and *Kampfgruppe von Luck* east of Epinal, 13 September 1944

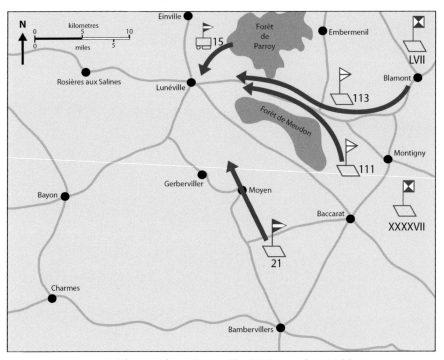

16. The attack on Luneville, 18 September 1944

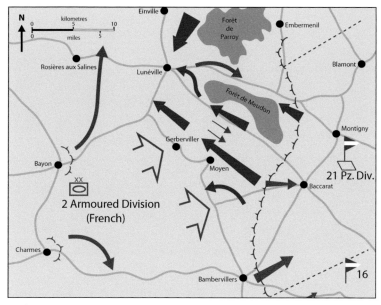

17. The American and French counter-attack after the failure at Luneville

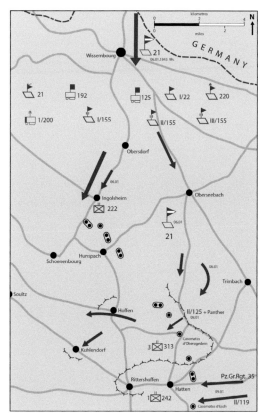

18. Attacks of *21. Panzer Division* 6-9 January, and *25. Panzergrenadier Division* on 9 January 1945

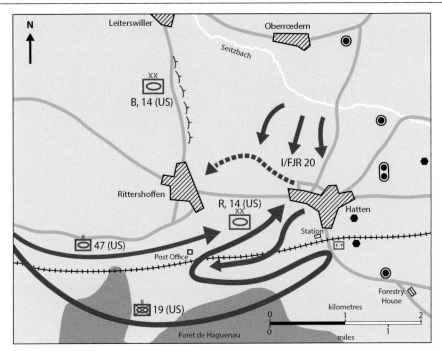

19. The battle for Hatten against the US 14th Armored Division, 13 January 1945

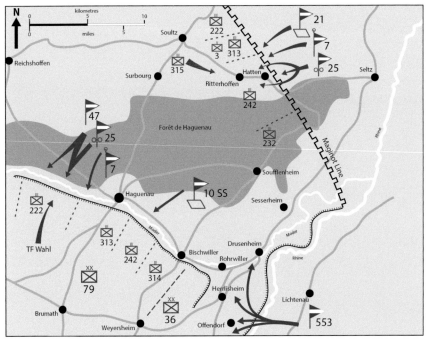

20. Development of the situation between 6 and 22 January 1945

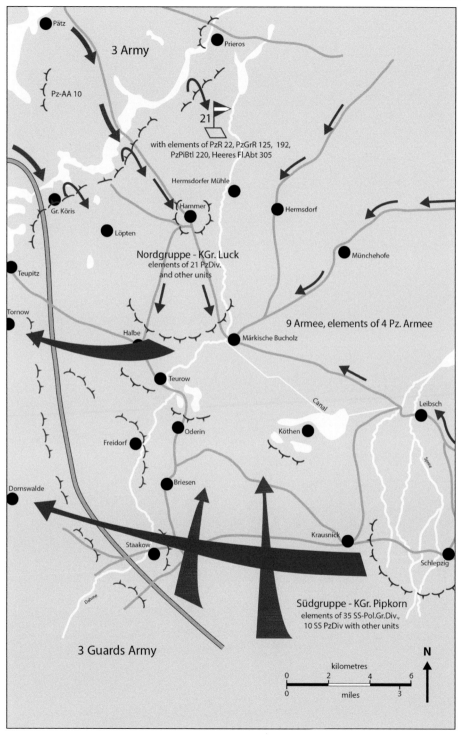

21. Preparations for the break-out, 25 April 1945